TRAVEL JOURNAL

First published in 2019 by Erin Rose Publishing

Text and illustration copyright © 2019 Erin Rose Publishing

Design: Julie Anson

THIS TRAVEL JOURNAL BELONGS TO:

....

AGE: ....

My Adventure To:

....

MY JOURNEY STARTS AT: ....

AND ENDS IN: ....

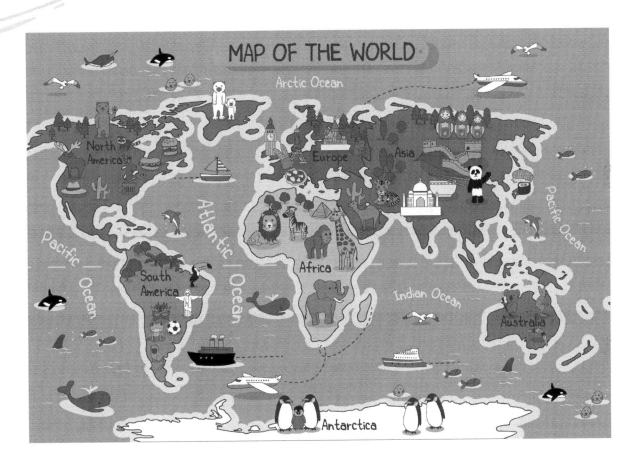

JANUARY	FEBRUARY	MARCH	APRIL	MAY	JUNE	JULY	AUGUST	SEPTEMBER	OCTOBER	NOVEMBER	DECEMBER

THE BEST ADVENTURE

HOW LONG IS THE JOURNEY? ....

HOW AM I TRAVELLING? ....

WHERE AM I STAYING? ....

WHO IS GOING? ....

WHAT WOULD I LIKE TO DO WHEN I GET THERE? ....

....

....

....

....

....

WHAT AM I MOST LOOKING FORWARD TO? ....

....

....

....

WHAT DO I NEED TO PACK? YOU CAN WRITE YOUR PACKING LIST BELOW:

....

....

....

....

....

....

....

....

....

....

....

....

DATE:........................... LOCATION: .... TODAY'S STAR RATING: ☆☆☆☆☆

TRAVELLED BY: ✈ □ 🚢 □ 🌀 □ 🪧 □ 🎈 □
PLANE   BOAT   ROAD   WALK   OTHER

WHERE DID I VISIT?

WHO WAS THERE?

WHAT I DISCOVERED?

WHO DID I MEET?

MY FAVOURITE THING WAS:

MY MOOD WAS 😄 □ 🙂 □ 😐 □ 🙁 □ 😎 □ 😴 □

WEATHER ☀ □ ⛅ □ 🌦 □ ⛈ □ 🌧 □ 🌨 □

PICTURE OF THE DAY

DRAW, SKETCH OR STICK-IN A PICTURE OR KEEPSAKE OF YOUR DAY.

DATE:........................ LOCATION:................................. TODAY'S STAR RATING: ☆☆☆☆☆

TRAVELLED BY: ✈ PLANE ☐ 🚢 BOAT ☐ 🛣 ROAD ☐ 🪧 WALK ☐ 🎈 OTHER ☐

WHERE DID I VISIT?

WHO WAS THERE?

WHAT I DISCOVERED?

WHO DID I MEET?

MY FAVOURITE THING WAS:

MY MOOD WAS 😄☐ 🙂☐ 😐☐ 🙁☐ 😎☐ 😴☐

WEATHER ☀☐ ⛅☐ 🌦☐ ⛈☐ 🌧☐ ❄☐

PICTURE OF THE DAY

DRAW, SKETCH OR STICK-IN A PICTURE OR KEEPSAKE OF YOUR DAY.

DATE:............................ LOCATION: .... TODAY'S STAR RATING: ☆☆☆☆☆

TRAVELLED BY: ✈ ☐ 🚢 ☐ 🛣 ☐ 🪧 ☐ 🎈 ☐
PLANE   BOAT   ROAD   WALK   OTHER

WHERE DID I VISIT?

WHO WAS THERE?

WHAT I DISCOVERED?

WHO DID I MEET?

MY FAVOURITE THING WAS:

MY MOOD WAS 😄☐ 🙂☐ 😐☐ ☹☐ 😎☐ 😴☐

WEATHER ☀☐ ⛅☐ 🌥☐ ⛈☐ 🌧☐ 🌨☐

PICTURE OF THE DAY

DRAW, SKETCH OR STICK-IN A PICTURE OR KEEPSAKE OF YOUR DAY.

DATE:.................... LOCATION:........................ TODAY'S STAR RATING: ☆☆☆☆☆

TRAVELLED BY: ✈ PLANE ☐ 🚢 BOAT ☐ 🛣 ROAD ☐ 🪧 WALK ☐ 🎈 OTHER ☐

WHERE DID I VISIT?

WHO WAS THERE?

WHAT I DISCOVERED?

WHO DID I MEET?

MY FAVOURITE THING WAS:

MY MOOD WAS 😄 ☐ 🙂 ☐ 😐 ☐ ☹ ☐ 😎 ☐ 😴 ☐

WEATHER ☀ ☐ ⛅ ☐ 🌦 ☐ ⛈ ☐ 🌧 ☐ 🌨 ☐

PICTURE OF THE DAY

DRAW, SKETCH OR STICK-IN A PICTURE OR KEEPSAKE OF YOUR DAY.

DATE:.................... LOCATION: .... TODAY'S STAR RATING: ☆☆☆☆☆

TRAVELLED BY: ✈ PLANE ☐ 🚢 BOAT ☐ 🛣 ROAD ☐ 🪧 WALK ☐ 🎈 OTHER ☐

WHERE DID I VISIT?

WHO WAS THERE?

WHAT I DISCOVERED?

WHO DID I MEET?

MY FAVOURITE THING WAS:

MY MOOD WAS 😄 ☐ 🙂 ☐ 😐 ☐ 🙁 ☐ 😎 ☐ 😴 ☐

WEATHER ☀ ☐ ⛅ ☐ 🌦 ☐ ⛈ ☐ 🌧 ☐ 🌨 ☐

PICTURE OF THE DAY

DRAW, SKETCH OR STICK-IN A PICTURE OR KEEPSAKE OF YOUR DAY.

DATE:................................ LOCATION:... TODAY'S STAR RATING: ☆☆☆☆☆

TRAVELLED BY: ✈ PLANE ☐ 🚢 BOAT ☐ 🛣 ROAD ☐ 🪧 WALK ☐ 🎈 OTHER ☐

WHERE DID I VISIT?

WHO WAS THERE?

WHAT I DISCOVERED?

WHO DID I MEET?

MY FAVOURITE THING WAS:

MY MOOD WAS 😄 ☐ 🙂 ☐ 😐 ☐ 🙁 ☐ 😎 ☐ 😴 ☐

WEATHER ☀ ☐ ⛅ ☐ 🌦 ☐ ⛈ ☐ 🌧 ☐ 🌨 ☐

PICTURE OF THE DAY

DRAW, SKETCH OR STICK-IN A PICTURE OR KEEPSAKE OF YOUR DAY.

DATE:.................................. LOCATION: .... TODAY'S STAR RATING: ☆☆☆☆☆

TRAVELLED BY: ✈ PLANE ☐ 🚢 BOAT ☐ 🛣 ROAD ☐ 🪧 WALK ☐ 🎈 OTHER ☐

WHERE DID I VISIT?

WHO WAS THERE?

WHAT I DISCOVERED?

WHO DID I MEET?

MY FAVOURITE THING WAS:

MY MOOD WAS 😄 ☐ 🙂 ☐ 😐 ☐ 🙁 ☐ 😎 ☐ 😴 ☐

WEATHER ☀ ☐ ⛅ ☐ 🌦 ☐ ⛈ ☐ 🌧 ☐ 🌨 ☐

PICTURE OF THE DAY

DRAW, SKETCH OR STICK-IN A PICTURE OR KEEPSAKE OF YOUR DAY.

DATE:............................ LOCATION:... TODAY'S STAR RATING: ☆☆☆☆☆

TRAVELLED BY: ✈ PLANE ☐   🚢 BOAT ☐   ROAD ☐   WALK ☐   OTHER ☐

WHERE DID I VISIT?

WHO WAS THERE?

WHAT I DISCOVERED?

WHO DID I MEET?

MY FAVOURITE THING WAS:

MY MOOD WAS   😄 ☐   🙂 ☐   😐 ☐   🙁 ☐   😎 ☐   😴 ☐

WEATHER   ☀ ☐   ⛅ ☐   🌦 ☐   ⛈ ☐   🌧 ☐   ❄ ☐

PICTURE OF THE DAY

DRAW, SKETCH OR STICK-IN A PICTURE OR KEEPSAKE OF YOUR DAY.

DATE:........................ LOCATION:.. TODAY'S STAR RATING: ☆☆☆☆☆

TRAVELLED BY: ✈ PLANE ☐ 🚢 BOAT ☐ 🚗 ROAD ☐ 🪧 WALK ☐ 🎈 OTHER ☐

WHERE DID I VISIT?

WHO WAS THERE?

WHAT I DISCOVERED?

WHO DID I MEET?

MY FAVOURITE THING WAS:

MY MOOD WAS 😄 ☐ 🙂 ☐ 😐 ☐ 🙁 ☐ 😎 ☐ 😴 ☐

WEATHER ☀ ☐ ⛅ ☐ 🌦 ☐ ⛈ ☐ 🌧 ☐ ❄ ☐

PICTURE OF THE DAY

DRAW, SKETCH OR STICK-IN A PICTURE OR KEEPSAKE OF YOUR DAY.

DATE:............................ LOCATION:... TODAY'S STAR RATING: ☆☆☆☆☆☆

TRAVELLED BY: ✈ ☐ 🚢 ☐ 🛣 ☐ 🪧 ☐ 🎈 ☐
PLANE   BOAT   ROAD   WALK   OTHER

WHERE DID I VISIT?

WHO WAS THERE?

WHAT I DISCOVERED?

WHO DID I MEET?

MY FAVOURITE THING WAS:

MY MOOD WAS 😄☐ 🙂☐ 😐☐ 🙁☐ 😎☐ 😴☐

WEATHER ☀☐ ⛅☐ 🌤☐ ⛈☐ 🌧☐ 🌨☐

PICTURE OF THE DAY

DRAW, SKETCH OR STICK-IN A PICTURE OR KEEPSAKE OF YOUR DAY.

DATE:................................. LOCATION: .... TODAY'S STAR RATING: ☆☆☆☆☆

TRAVELLED BY: ✈ □ 🚢 □ 🛣 □ 🪧 □ 🎈 □
              PLANE   BOAT   ROAD   WALK   OTHER

WHERE DID I VISIT?

WHO WAS THERE?

WHAT I DISCOVERED?

WHO DID I MEET?

MY FAVOURITE THING WAS:

MY MOOD WAS 😄 □ 🙂 □ 😐 □ 🙁 □ 😎 □ 😴 □

WEATHER ☀ □ ⛅ □ 🌦 □ ⛈ □ 🌧 □ 🌨 □

PICTURE OF THE DAY

DRAW, SKETCH OR STICK-IN A PICTURE OR KEEPSAKE OF YOUR DAY.

DATE:.................... LOCATION: .... TODAY'S STAR RATING: ☆☆☆☆☆

TRAVELLED BY: ✈ ☐ 🚢 ☐ 🛣 ☐ 🪧 ☐ 🎈 ☐
PLANE   BOAT   ROAD   WALK   OTHER

WHERE DID I VISIT?

WHO WAS THERE?

WHAT I DISCOVERED?

WHO DID I MEET?

MY FAVOURITE THING WAS:

MY MOOD WAS 😄☐ 🙂☐ 😐☐ 🙁☐ 😎☐ 😴☐

WEATHER ☀☐ ⛅☐ 🌥☐ ⛈☐ 🌧☐ 🌨☐

PICTURE OF THE DAY

DRAW, SKETCH OR STICK-IN A PICTURE OR KEEPSAKE OF YOUR DAY.

DATE:...................... LOCATION:.. TODAY'S STAR RATING: ☆☆☆☆☆

TRAVELLED BY: PLANE ☐ BOAT ☐ ROAD ☐ WALK ☐ OTHER ☐

WHERE DID I VISIT?

WHO WAS THERE?

WHAT I DISCOVERED?

WHO DID I MEET?

MY FAVOURITE THING WAS:

MY MOOD WAS 😄☐ 🙂☐ 😐☐ 🙁☐ 😎☐ 😴☐

WEATHER ☀️☐ ⛅☐ 🌦️☐ ⛈️☐ 🌧️☐ 🌨️☐

PICTURE OF THE DAY

DRAW, SKETCH OR STICK-IN A PICTURE OR KEEPSAKE OF YOUR DAY.

DATE:.................................... LOCATION:... TODAY'S STAR RATING: ☆☆☆☆☆

TRAVELLED BY: ✈ ☐   🚢 ☐   🛣 ☐   🪧 ☐   🎈 ☐
             PLANE   BOAT   ROAD   WALK   OTHER

WHERE DID I VISIT?

WHO WAS THERE?

WHAT I DISCOVERED?

WHO DID I MEET?

MY FAVOURITE THING WAS:

MY MOOD WAS 😄 ☐ 🙂 ☐ 😐 ☐ 🙁 ☐ 😎 ☐ 😴 ☐

WEATHER ☀ ☐ 🌤 ☐ 🌥 ☐ ⛈ ☐ 🌧 ☐ 🌨 ☐

PICTURE OF THE DAY

DRAW, SKETCH OR STICK-IN A PICTURE OR KEEPSAKE OF YOUR DAY.

DATE:........................ LOCATION:.. TODAY'S STAR RATING: ☆☆☆☆☆

TRAVELLED BY:
PLANE ☐   BOAT ☐   ROAD ☐   WALK ☐   OTHER ☐

WHERE DID I VISIT?

WHO WAS THERE?

WHAT I DISCOVERED?

WHO DID I MEET?

MY FAVOURITE THING WAS:

MY MOOD WAS 😄☐ 🙂☐ 😐☐ 🙁☐ 😎☐ 😴☐

WEATHER ☀️☐ ⛅☐ 🌦️☐ ⛈️☐ 🌧️☐ ❄️☐

PICTURE OF THE DAY

DRAW, SKETCH OR STICK-IN A PICTURE OR KEEPSAKE OF YOUR DAY.

DATE:.................... LOCATION:.............................. TODAY'S STAR RATING: ☆☆☆☆☆

TRAVELLED BY: ✈ PLANE ☐ 🚢 BOAT ☐ 🛣 ROAD ☐ 🪧 WALK ☐ 🎈 OTHER ☐

WHERE DID I VISIT?

WHO WAS THERE?

WHAT I DISCOVERED?

WHO DID I MEET?

MY FAVOURITE THING WAS:

MY MOOD WAS 😄 ☐ 🙂 ☐ 😐 ☐ 🙁 ☐ 😎 ☐ 😴 ☐

WEATHER ☀ ☐ ⛅ ☐ 🌦 ☐ ⛈ ☐ 🌧 ☐ ❄ ☐

PICTURE OF THE DAY

DRAW, SKETCH OR STICK-IN A PICTURE OR KEEPSAKE OF YOUR DAY.

DATE:.................... LOCATION:............................. TODAY'S STAR RATING: ☆☆☆☆☆

TRAVELLED BY: ✈ PLANE ☐ 🚢 BOAT ☐ 🛣 ROAD ☐ 🪧 WALK ☐ 🎈 OTHER ☐

WHERE DID I VISIT?

WHO WAS THERE?

WHAT I DISCOVERED?

WHO DID I MEET?

MY FAVOURITE THING WAS:

MY MOOD WAS 😄 ☐ 🙂 ☐ 😐 ☐ ☹ ☐ 😎 ☐ 😴 ☐

WEATHER ☀ ☐ ⛅ ☐ 🌤 ☐ ⛈ ☐ 🌧 ☐ 🌨 ☐

PICTURE OF THE DAY

DRAW, SKETCH OR STICK-IN A PICTURE OR KEEPSAKE OF YOUR DAY.

DATE:.............................. LOCATION:... TODAY'S STAR RATING: ☆☆☆☆☆

TRAVELLED BY: ✈ PLANE ☐   🚢 BOAT ☐   🛣 ROAD ☐   🪧 WALK ☐   🎈 OTHER ☐

WHERE DID I VISIT?

WHO WAS THERE?

WHAT I DISCOVERED?

WHO DID I MEET?

MY FAVOURITE THING WAS:

MY MOOD WAS 😄 ☐   🙂 ☐   😐 ☐   🙁 ☐   😎 ☐   😴 ☐

WEATHER ☀ ☐   ⛅ ☐   🌦 ☐   ⛈ ☐   🌧 ☐   🌨 ☐

PICTURE OF THE DAY

DRAW, SKETCH OR STICK-IN A PICTURE OR KEEPSAKE OF YOUR DAY.

DATE:............................ LOCATION:... TODAY'S STAR RATING: ☆☆☆☆☆

TRAVELLED BY: ✈ ☐   🚢 ☐   🛣 ☐   🪧 ☐   🎈 ☐
              PLANE   BOAT   ROAD   WALK   OTHER

WHERE DID I VISIT?

WHO WAS THERE?

WHAT I DISCOVERED?

WHO DID I MEET?

MY FAVOURITE THING WAS:

MY MOOD WAS 😄 ☐ 🙂 ☐ 😐 ☐ 🙁 ☐ 😎 ☐ 😴 ☐

WEATHER ☀ ☐ ⛅ ☐ 🌦 ☐ ⛈ ☐ 🌧 ☐ ❄ ☐

PICTURE OF THE DAY

DRAW, SKETCH OR STICK-IN A PICTURE OR KEEPSAKE OF YOUR DAY.

DATE:.................... LOCATION:........................... TODAY'S STAR RATING: ☆☆☆☆☆

TRAVELLED BY: ✈ PLANE ☐ 🚢 BOAT ☐ 🛣 ROAD ☐ 🪧 WALK ☐ 🎈 OTHER ☐

WHERE DID I VISIT?

WHO WAS THERE?

WHAT I DISCOVERED?

WHO DID I MEET?

MY FAVOURITE THING WAS:

MY MOOD WAS 😄 ☐ 🙂 ☐ 😐 ☐ ☹ ☐ 😎 ☐ 😴 ☐

WEATHER ☀ ☐ ⛅ ☐ 🌦 ☐ ⛈ ☐ 🌧 ☐ 🌨 ☐

PICTURE OF THE DAY

DRAW, SKETCH OR STICK-IN A PICTURE OR KEEPSAKE OF YOUR DAY.

DATE:............................ LOCATION:.. TODAY'S STAR RATING: ☆☆☆☆☆

TRAVELLED BY: ✈ □ PLANE 🚢 □ BOAT 🛤 □ ROAD 🪧 □ WALK 🎈 □ OTHER

WHERE DID I VISIT?

WHO WAS THERE?

WHAT I DISCOVERED?

WHO DID I MEET?

MY FAVOURITE THING WAS:

MY MOOD WAS 😄 □ 🙂 □ 😐 □ 🙁 □ 😎 □ 😴 □

WEATHER ☀ □ ⛅ □ 🌦 □ ⛈ □ 🌧 □ 🌨 □

PICTURE OF THE DAY

DRAW, SKETCH OR STICK-IN A PICTURE OR KEEPSAKE OF YOUR DAY.

DATE:........................ LOCATION:.. TODAY'S STAR RATING: ☆☆☆☆☆

TRAVELLED BY: ✈ PLANE ☐ 🚢 BOAT ☐ 🚗 ROAD ☐ 🪧 WALK ☐ 🎈 OTHER ☐

WHERE DID I VISIT?

WHO WAS THERE?

WHAT I DISCOVERED?

WHO DID I MEET?

MY FAVOURITE THING WAS:

MY MOOD WAS 😄☐ 🙂☐ 😐☐ 🙁☐ 😎☐ 😴☐

WEATHER ☀☐ ⛅☐ 🌦☐ ⛈☐ 🌧☐ 🌨☐

PICTURE OF THE DAY

DRAW, SKETCH OR STICK-IN A PICTURE OR KEEPSAKE OF YOUR DAY.

DATE:.................... LOCATION:.......................... TODAY'S STAR RATING: ☆☆☆☆☆

TRAVELLED BY: ✈ ☐   🚢 ☐   🛣 ☐   🪧 ☐   🎈 ☐
              PLANE   BOAT   ROAD   WALK   OTHER

WHERE DID I VISIT?

WHO WAS THERE?

WHAT I DISCOVERED?

WHO DID I MEET?

MY FAVOURITE THING WAS:

MY MOOD WAS 😄 ☐ 🙂 ☐ 😐 ☐ 🙁 ☐ 😎 ☐ 😴 ☐

WEATHER ☀ ☐ ⛅ ☐ 🌥 ☐ ⛈ ☐ 🌧 ☐ 🌨 ☐

PICTURE OF THE DAY

DRAW, SKETCH OR STICK-IN A PICTURE OR KEEPSAKE OF YOUR DAY.

DATE:........................ LOCATION: .... TODAY'S STAR RATING: ☆☆☆☆☆

TRAVELLED BY: ✈ ☐   🚢 ☐   🌋 ☐   🪧 ☐   🎈 ☐
PLANE   BOAT   ROAD   WALK   OTHER

WHERE DID I VISIT?

WHO WAS THERE?

WHAT I DISCOVERED?

WHO DID I MEET?

MY FAVOURITE THING WAS:

MY MOOD WAS   😄 ☐   🙂 ☐   😐 ☐   🙁 ☐   😎 ☐   😴 ☐

WEATHER   ☀ ☐   ⛅ ☐   🌥 ☐   ⛈ ☐   🌧 ☐   🌨 ☐

PICTURE OF THE DAY

DRAW, SKETCH OR STICK-IN A PICTURE OR KEEPSAKE OF YOUR DAY.

DATE:........................ LOCATION:.. TODAY'S STAR RATING: ☆☆☆☆☆

TRAVELLED BY: ✈ ☐ 🚢 ☐ 🛣 ☐ 🪧 ☐ 🎈 ☐
               PLANE   BOAT   ROAD   WALK   OTHER

WHERE DID I VISIT?

WHO WAS THERE?

WHAT I DISCOVERED?

WHO DID I MEET?

MY FAVOURITE THING WAS:

MY MOOD WAS 😄 ☐ 🙂 ☐ 😐 ☐ 🙁 ☐ 😎 ☐ 😴 ☐

WEATHER ☀ ☐ ⛅ ☐ 🌦 ☐ ⛈ ☐ 🌧 ☐ 🌨 ☐

PICTURE OF THE DAY

DRAW, SKETCH OR STICK-IN A PICTURE OR KEEPSAKE OF YOUR DAY.

DATE: .... LOCATION: .... TODAY'S STAR RATING: ☆☆☆☆☆

TRAVELLED BY: ✈ PLANE ☐ 🚢 BOAT ☐ 🛣 ROAD ☐ 🪧 WALK ☐ 🎈 OTHER ☐

WHERE DID I VISIT?

WHO WAS THERE?

WHAT I DISCOVERED?

WHO DID I MEET?

MY FAVOURITE THING WAS:

MY MOOD WAS 😄 ☐ 🙂 ☐ 😐 ☐ 🙁 ☐ 😎 ☐ 😴 ☐

WEATHER ☀ ☐ ⛅ ☐ 🌦 ☐ ⛈ ☐ 🌧 ☐ ❄ ☐

PICTURE OF THE DAY

DRAW, SKETCH OR STICK-IN A PICTURE OR KEEPSAKE OF YOUR DAY.

DATE:...................... LOCATION:..................................... TODAY'S STAR RATING: ☆☆☆☆☆

TRAVELLED BY: ✈ PLANE ☐ 🚢 BOAT ☐ 🛣 ROAD ☐ 🪧 WALK ☐ 🎈 OTHER ☐

WHERE DID I VISIT?

WHO WAS THERE?

WHAT I DISCOVERED?

WHO DID I MEET?

MY FAVOURITE THING WAS:

MY MOOD WAS 😄 ☐ 🙂 ☐ 😐 ☐ 🙁 ☐ 😎 ☐ 😴 ☐

WEATHER ☀ ☐ ⛅ ☐ 🌥 ☐ ⛈ ☐ 🌧 ☐ 🌨 ☐

PICTURE OF THE DAY

DRAW, SKETCH OR STICK-IN A PICTURE OR KEEPSAKE OF YOUR DAY.

DATE:.................... LOCATION:.................................. TODAY'S STAR RATING: ☆☆☆☆☆

TRAVELLED BY: ✈ PLANE ☐ 🚢 BOAT ☐ 🛣 ROAD ☐ 🪧 WALK ☐ 🎈 OTHER ☐

WHERE DID I VISIT?

WHO WAS THERE?

WHAT I DISCOVERED?

WHO DID I MEET?

MY FAVOURITE THING WAS:

MY MOOD WAS 😄 ☐ 🙂 ☐ 😐 ☐ 🙁 ☐ 😎 ☐ 😴 ☐

WEATHER ☀ ☐ ⛅ ☐ 🌥 ☐ ⛈ ☐ 🌧 ☐ 🌨 ☐

PICTURE OF THE DAY

DRAW, SKETCH OR STICK-IN A PICTURE OR KEEPSAKE OF YOUR DAY.

DATE: .... LOCATION: .... TODAY'S STAR RATING: ☆☆☆☆☆

TRAVELLED BY: ✈ □   🚢 □   🛣 □   🪧 □   🎈 □
PLANE   BOAT   ROAD   WALK   OTHER

WHERE DID I VISIT?

WHO WAS THERE?

WHAT I DISCOVERED?

WHO DID I MEET?

MY FAVOURITE THING WAS:

MY MOOD WAS 😄 □ 🙂 □ 😐 □ 🙁 □ 😎 □ 😴 □

WEATHER ☀ □ ⛅ □ 🌥 □ ⛈ □ ☁ □ 🌨 □

PICTURE OF THE DAY

DRAW, SKETCH OR STICK-IN A PICTURE OR KEEPSAKE OF YOUR DAY.

DATE:........................ LOCATION:.. TODAY'S STAR RATING: ☆☆☆☆☆

TRAVELLED BY: ✈ □ 🚢 □ 🛣 □ 🪧 □ 🎈 □
PLANE   BOAT   ROAD   WALK   OTHER

WHERE DID I VISIT?

WHO WAS THERE?

WHAT I DISCOVERED?

WHO DID I MEET?

MY FAVOURITE THING WAS:

MY MOOD WAS 😄 □ 🙂 □ 😐 □ 🙁 □ 😎 □ 😴 □

WEATHER ☀ □ ⛅ □ 🌥 □ ⛈ □ 🌧 □ 🌨 □

PICTURE OF THE DAY

DRAW, SKETCH OR STICK-IN A PICTURE OR KEEPSAKE OF YOUR DAY.

DATE:........................ LOCATION: .... TODAY'S STAR RATING: ☆☆☆☆☆

TRAVELLED BY: ✈ ☐ 🚢 ☐ 🛣 ☐ 🪧 ☐ 🎈 ☐
PLANE   BOAT   ROAD   WALK   OTHER

WHERE DID I VISIT?

WHO WAS THERE?

WHAT I DISCOVERED?

WHO DID I MEET?

MY FAVOURITE THING WAS:

MY MOOD WAS 😄☐ 🙂☐ 😐☐ ☹☐ 😎☐ 😴☐

WEATHER ☀☐ ⛅☐ 🌥☐ ⛈☐ 🌧☐ 🌨☐

PICTURE OF THE DAY

DRAW, SKETCH OR STICK-IN A PICTURE OR KEEPSAKE OF YOUR DAY.

DATE:.................. LOCATION:..................................... TODAY'S STAR RATING: ☆☆☆☆☆

TRAVELLED BY: ✈️ ☐   🚢 ☐   🛣️ ☐   🪧 ☐   🎈 ☐
              PLANE   BOAT   ROAD   WALK   OTHER

WHERE DID I VISIT?

WHO WAS THERE?

WHAT I DISCOVERED?

WHO DID I MEET?

MY FAVOURITE THING WAS:

MY MOOD WAS 😄 ☐ 🙂 ☐ 😐 ☐ 🙁 ☐ 😎 ☐ 😴 ☐

WEATHER ☀️ ☐ ⛅ ☐ 🌦️ ☐ ⛈️ ☐ 🌧️ ☐ 🌨️ ☐

PICTURE OF THE DAY

DRAW, SKETCH OR STICK-IN A PICTURE OR KEEPSAKE OF YOUR DAY.

DATE:.................... LOCATION:.............................. TODAY'S STAR RATING: ☆☆☆☆☆

TRAVELLED BY: ✈ □ 🚢 □ ROAD □ WALK □ OTHER □
PLANE   BOAT   ROAD   WALK   OTHER

WHERE DID I VISIT?

WHO WAS THERE?

WHAT I DISCOVERED?

WHO DID I MEET?

MY FAVOURITE THING WAS:

MY MOOD WAS 😄 □ 🙂 □ 😐 □ ☹ □ 😎 □ 😴 □

WEATHER ☀ □ ⛅ □ 🌦 □ ⛈ □ ☁ □ 🌨 □

PICTURE OF THE DAY

DRAW, SKETCH OR STICK-IN A PICTURE OR KEEPSAKE OF YOUR DAY.

DATE:.................... LOCATION: .... TODAY'S STAR RATING: ☆☆☆☆☆

TRAVELLED BY: ✈ ☐ 🚢 ☐ 🛣 ☐ 🪧 ☐ 🎈 ☐
PLANE   BOAT   ROAD   WALK   OTHER

WHERE DID I VISIT?

WHO WAS THERE?

WHAT I DISCOVERED?

WHO DID I MEET?

MY FAVOURITE THING WAS:

MY MOOD WAS 😄☐ 🙂☐ 😐☐ 🙁☐ 😎☐ 😴☐

WEATHER ☀☐ ⛅☐ 🌥☐ ⛈☐ 🌧☐ 🌨☐

PICTURE OF THE DAY

DRAW, SKETCH OR STICK-IN A PICTURE OR KEEPSAKE OF YOUR DAY.

DATE:.................... LOCATION:............................. TODAY'S STAR RATING: ☆☆☆☆☆

TRAVELLED BY: ✈ PLANE ☐ 🚢 BOAT ☐ 🛤 ROAD ☐ 🪧 WALK ☐ 🎈 OTHER ☐

WHERE DID I VISIT?

WHO WAS THERE?

WHAT I DISCOVERED?

WHO DID I MEET?

MY FAVOURITE THING WAS:

MY MOOD WAS 😄 ☐ 🙂 ☐ 😐 ☐ 🙁 ☐ 😎 ☐ 😴 ☐

WEATHER ☀ ☐ ☁ ☐ 🌦 ☐ ⛈ ☐ 🌧 ☐ 🌨 ☐

PICTURE OF THE DAY

DRAW, SKETCH OR STICK-IN A PICTURE OR KEEPSAKE OF YOUR DAY.

DATE:.................... LOCATION:.. TODAY'S STAR RATING: ☆☆☆☆☆

TRAVELLED BY: ✈ PLANE ☐ 🚢 BOAT ☐ 🛣 ROAD ☐ 🚏 WALK ☐ 🎈 OTHER ☐

WHERE DID I VISIT?

WHO WAS THERE?

WHAT I DISCOVERED?

WHO DID I MEET?

MY FAVOURITE THING WAS:

MY MOOD WAS 😄 ☐ 🙂 ☐ 😐 ☐ ☹ ☐ 😎 ☐ 😴 ☐

WEATHER ☀ ☐ ⛅ ☐ 🌦 ☐ ⛈ ☐ ☁ ☐ 🌨 ☐

PICTURE OF THE DAY

DRAW, SKETCH OR STICK-IN A PICTURE OR KEEPSAKE OF YOUR DAY.

DATE:............................ LOCATION:.. TODAY'S STAR RATING: ☆ ☆ ☆ ☆ ☆

TRAVELLED BY: ✈ □   🚢 □   🛣 □   🪧 □   🎈 □
PLANE   BOAT   ROAD   WALK   OTHER

WHERE DID I VISIT?

WHO WAS THERE?

WHAT I DISCOVERED?

WHO DID I MEET?

MY FAVOURITE THING WAS:

MY MOOD WAS 😄 □ 🙂 □ 😐 □ 🙁 □ 😎 □ 😴 □

WEATHER ☀ □ 🌤 □ ⛅ □ ⛈ □ 🌧 □ ❄ □

PICTURE OF THE DAY

DRAW, SKETCH OR STICK-IN A PICTURE OR KEEPSAKE OF YOUR DAY.

DATE:........................ LOCATION:... TODAY'S STAR RATING: ☆☆☆☆☆

TRAVELLED BY: 🛩 ☐   🚢 ☐   🌪 ☐   🚏 ☐   🎈 ☐
            PLANE   BOAT   ROAD   WALK   OTHER

WHERE DID I VISIT?

WHO WAS THERE?

WHAT I DISCOVERED?

WHO DID I MEET?

MY FAVOURITE THING WAS:

MY MOOD WAS 😄 ☐ 🙂 ☐ 😐 ☐ 🙁 ☐ 😎 ☐ 😴 ☐

WEATHER ☀ ☐ ⛅ ☐ ☁ ☐ ⛈ ☐ 🌧 ☐ 🌨 ☐

PICTURE OF THE DAY

DRAW, SKETCH OR STICK-IN A PICTURE OR KEEPSAKE OF YOUR DAY.

DATE:................................ LOCATION: .... TODAY'S STAR RATING: ☆☆☆☆☆

TRAVELLED BY: ✈ ☐ ⛴ ☐ 🛣 ☐ 🪧 ☐ 🎈 ☐
PLANE   BOAT   ROAD   WALK   OTHER

WHERE DID I VISIT?

WHO WAS THERE?

WHAT I DISCOVERED?

WHO DID I MEET?

MY FAVOURITE THING WAS:

MY MOOD WAS 😄 ☐ 🙂 ☐ 😐 ☐ 🙁 ☐ 😎 ☐ 😴 ☐

WEATHER   ☀ ☐ ⛅ ☐ 🌦 ☐ ⛈ ☐ 🌧 ☐ 🌨 ☐

PICTURE OF THE DAY

DRAW, SKETCH OR STICK-IN A PICTURE OR KEEPSAKE OF YOUR DAY.

DATE: .... LOCATION: .... TODAY'S STAR RATING: ☆☆☆☆☆

TRAVELLED BY: ✈ ☐ 🚢 ☐ 🛣 ☐ 🪧 ☐ 🎈 ☐
PLANE BOAT ROAD WALK OTHER

WHERE DID I VISIT?

WHO WAS THERE?

WHAT I DISCOVERED?

WHO DID I MEET?

MY FAVOURITE THING WAS:

MY MOOD WAS 😄 ☐ 🙂 ☐ 😐 ☐ ☹ ☐ 😎 ☐ 😴 ☐

WEATHER ☀ ☐ ⛅ ☐ 🌥 ☐ ⛈ ☐ 🌧 ☐ 🌨 ☐

PICTURE OF THE DAY

DRAW, SKETCH OR STICK-IN A PICTURE OR KEEPSAKE OF YOUR DAY.

DATE:.............................. LOCATION:.. TODAY'S STAR RATING: ☆☆☆☆☆

TRAVELLED BY: ✈ ☐ 🚢 ☐ 🛣 ☐ 🪧 ☐ 🎈 ☐
             PLANE   BOAT   ROAD   WALK   OTHER

WHERE DID I VISIT?

WHO WAS THERE?

WHAT I DISCOVERED?

WHO DID I MEET?

MY FAVOURITE THING WAS:

MY MOOD WAS 😄 ☐ 🙂 ☐ 😐 ☐ 🙁 ☐ 😎 ☐ 😴 ☐

WEATHER ☀ ☐ ⛅ ☐ 🌥 ☐ ⛈ ☐ 🌧 ☐ 🌨 ☐

PICTURE OF THE DAY

DRAW, SKETCH OR STICK-IN A PICTURE OR KEEPSAKE OF YOUR DAY.

DATE: .... LOCATION: .... TODAY'S STAR RATING: ☆☆☆☆☆

TRAVELLED BY: ✈ ☐ 🚢 ☐ 🛣 ☐ 🪧 ☐ 🎈 ☐
PLANE   BOAT   ROAD   WALK   OTHER

WHERE DID I VISIT?

WHO WAS THERE?

WHAT I DISCOVERED?

WHO DID I MEET?

MY FAVOURITE THING WAS:

MY MOOD WAS 😄 ☐ 🙂 ☐ 😐 ☐ 🙁 ☐ 😎 ☐ 😴 ☐

WEATHER ☀ ☐ ⛅ ☐ 🌦 ☐ ⛈ ☐ 🌧 ☐ 🌨 ☐

PICTURE OF THE DAY

DRAW, SKETCH OR STICK-IN A PICTURE OR KEEPSAKE OF YOUR DAY.

DATE: .... LOCATION: .... TODAY'S STAR RATING: ☆☆☆☆☆

TRAVELLED BY: ✈ PLANE ☐ 🚢 BOAT ☐ 🛤 ROAD ☐ 🪧 WALK ☐ 🎈 OTHER ☐

WHERE DID I VISIT?

WHO WAS THERE?

WHAT I DISCOVERED?

WHO DID I MEET?

MY FAVOURITE THING WAS:

MY MOOD WAS 😄 ☐ 🙂 ☐ 😐 ☐ 🙁 ☐ 😎 ☐ 😴 ☐

WEATHER ☀ ☐ ⛅ ☐ 🌦 ☐ ⛈ ☐ ☁ ☐ 🌨 ☐

PICTURE OF THE DAY

DRAW, SKETCH OR STICK-IN A PICTURE OR KEEPSAKE OF YOUR DAY.

DATE:........................   LOCATION:...   TODAY'S STAR RATING: ☆☆☆☆☆

TRAVELLED BY: ✈ PLANE ☐   🚢 BOAT ☐   🛣 ROAD ☐   🪧 WALK ☐   🎈 OTHER ☐

WHERE DID I VISIT?

WHO WAS THERE?

WHAT I DISCOVERED?

WHO DID I MEET?

MY FAVOURITE THING WAS:

MY MOOD WAS   😄 ☐   🙂 ☐   😐 ☐   🙁 ☐   😎 ☐   😴 ☐

WEATHER   ☀ ☐   🌤 ☐   🌦 ☐   ⛈ ☐   🌧 ☐   🌨 ☐

PICTURE OF THE DAY

DRAW, SKETCH OR STICK-IN A PICTURE OR KEEPSAKE OF YOUR DAY.

DATE: .... LOCATION: .... TODAY'S STAR RATING: ☆ ☆ ☆ ☆ ☆

TRAVELLED BY: ✈ □ 🚢 □ 🛣 □ 🪧 □ 🎈 □
PLANE   BOAT   ROAD   WALK   OTHER

WHERE DID I VISIT?

WHO WAS THERE?

WHAT I DISCOVERED?

WHO DID I MEET?

MY FAVOURITE THING WAS:

MY MOOD WAS 😄 □ 🙂 □ 😐 □ ☹ □ 😎 □ 😴 □

WEATHER ☀ □ ⛅ □ 🌦 □ ⛈ □ 🌧 □ 🌨 □

PICTURE OF THE DAY

DRAW, SKETCH OR STICK-IN A PICTURE OR KEEPSAKE OF YOUR DAY.

DATE:................................... LOCATION:.. TODAY'S STAR RATING: ☆ ☆ ☆ ☆ ☆

TRAVELLED BY: ✈ ☐   🚢 ☐   🛣 ☐   🪧 ☐   🎈 ☐
PLANE   BOAT   ROAD   WALK   OTHER

WHERE DID I VISIT?

WHO WAS THERE?

WHAT I DISCOVERED?

WHO DID I MEET?

MY FAVOURITE THING WAS:

MY MOOD WAS 😄 ☐ 🙂 ☐ 😐 ☐ 🙁 ☐ 😎 ☐ 😴 ☐

WEATHER ☀ ☐ ⛅ ☐ 🌥 ☐ ⛈ ☐ 🌧 ☐ 🌨 ☐

PICTURE OF THE DAY

DRAW, SKETCH OR STICK-IN A PICTURE OR KEEPSAKE OF YOUR DAY.

THE BEST TRIP

40385801R00058

Made in the USA
San Bernardino, CA
26 June 2019